A Lady Has the Floor

Belva Lockwood Speaks Out for Women's Rights

EQUAL RIGHTS FOR ALL

KATE HANNIGAN

ILLUSTRATED BY ALISON JAY

CALKINS CREEK

AN IMPRINT OF HIGHLIGHTS

Honesdale, Pennsylvania

Belva Bennett liked to race through fields, chase stray cows, and tend to chores from sunup to sundown with her brother and sisters. Bright-eyed and dirty-faced, Belva was "not afraid of snakes or rats or *nothing*." She could hold her own with any of the boys in Niagara County, New York.

Belva chased her dreams the same way she rode her horse

Bold! Determined! Strong!

Belva was smart, too! At fourteen, she untied her girlish braids and took a job as head teacher at the one-room schoolhouse. Belva led the students in spelling and sums. But when payday came, she was shocked to discover that her salary was half what male teachers earned.

Are women not worth the same as men?
Belva spent her whole life asking that question.

"Has God given to one half of his creatures talents, and gifts that are but as a mockery—wings but not to fly?"

Belva set her sights on a teaching degree, but her father disapproved. *College is for men!*
No women allowed! Belva packed her bags, wanting to see for herself. Though the school
discouraged it, Belva enrolled in math, science, and politics—classes typically limited to men.
When she completed college in 1857, Belva graduated with honors!

Striking out on her own, Belva taught at schools around New York. But she didn't like how girls were treated. Teachers wouldn't let girls speak in front of the school or participate in physical activity.

Chin up! Voice steady!

Belva remembered the reformers she'd heard speak during college.

Susan B. Anthony and Elizabeth Cady Stanton demanded equal rights for women. Maybe, Belva thought, those rights should begin with girls.

She tried an experiment. Belva invited her female students onstage beside the boys to deliver speeches while the whole school listened.

It proved a success! So Belva brainstormed with Susan B. Anthony to hammer out a bigger plan. Together they pushed for every school in New York to teach public speaking to boys *and* girls.

Belva didn't stop there. Remembering her rough-and-tumble farm days, she insisted on physical activities for girls, just like for boys. *Gymnastics! Nature hikes! Ice-skating!* Soon all her students were allowed to tumble, trek, glide, and play.

"I believe that a woman should be equal to a man. . . . Both should be independent."

Belva hungered for an even bigger stage. After the Civil War, she believed a new day was dawning in the nation's capital. America was rebuilding, and fresh ideas were pushing stale ones aside. So she waved good-bye to New York and moved to Washington, D.C., lugging her tapestry bags, heavy trunks, and big dreams.

Equal pay for equal work!
Women should have the vote!

Eager to fight for justice and fairness, Belva applied to law school. But she quickly learned those doors were closed to women.

Belva kept knocking.

She heard *No!* again and again, until finally one law school said *YES!* Belva and fourteen other women pushed through the doors and into the classrooms.

Her lamp burning late into the night, Belva read, wrote, and memorized. But the school blocked women from attending lectures and studying with men. One by one, the other women began to quit. When it came time for graduation, the male students refused to sit beside the remaining women onstage.

No women! Embarrassing! Ridiculous!

Belva hung on, even when the school refused to present her with
a diploma. "I was not to be squelched so easily."

In September 1873, Belva wrote a letter to the president of the university.
His name was Ulysses S. Grant, and he was also president of the United States. "I have
passed through the curriculum of study in this school, and am entitled to, and *demand*,
my diploma."

Days later, Belva opened her door to a special delivery. It was her diploma, with President Grant's swooping signature clear to see. Belva stood proud as one of the first women in America to earn a law degree!

An attorney now, Belva helped poor widows, Civil War veterans, and freed slaves fight for what they deserved. But certain high courts refused to let women lawyers argue.

Bang, bang! sounded the gavel.

SIT DOWN! shouted the judge.

"Fight, fight, fight everlastingly—not with your claws and fists, but with your wits."

Belva protested to the U.S. Supreme Court, the highest court in the land.
The justices there told her what she'd already heard before: *No women allowed!*
Belva refused to be silenced.

Belva battled for a woman's right to practice law in any court. "Nothing was too daring for me to attempt." Over five years, she drafted new rules, lobbied congressmen to her side, and argued for equality.

In 1879, Belva won! Standing tall before the marble columns and the nine black-robed justices, Belva filled the chamber of the Supreme Court—for the first time in America's history—with a woman's voice.

Bold! Determined! Strong!

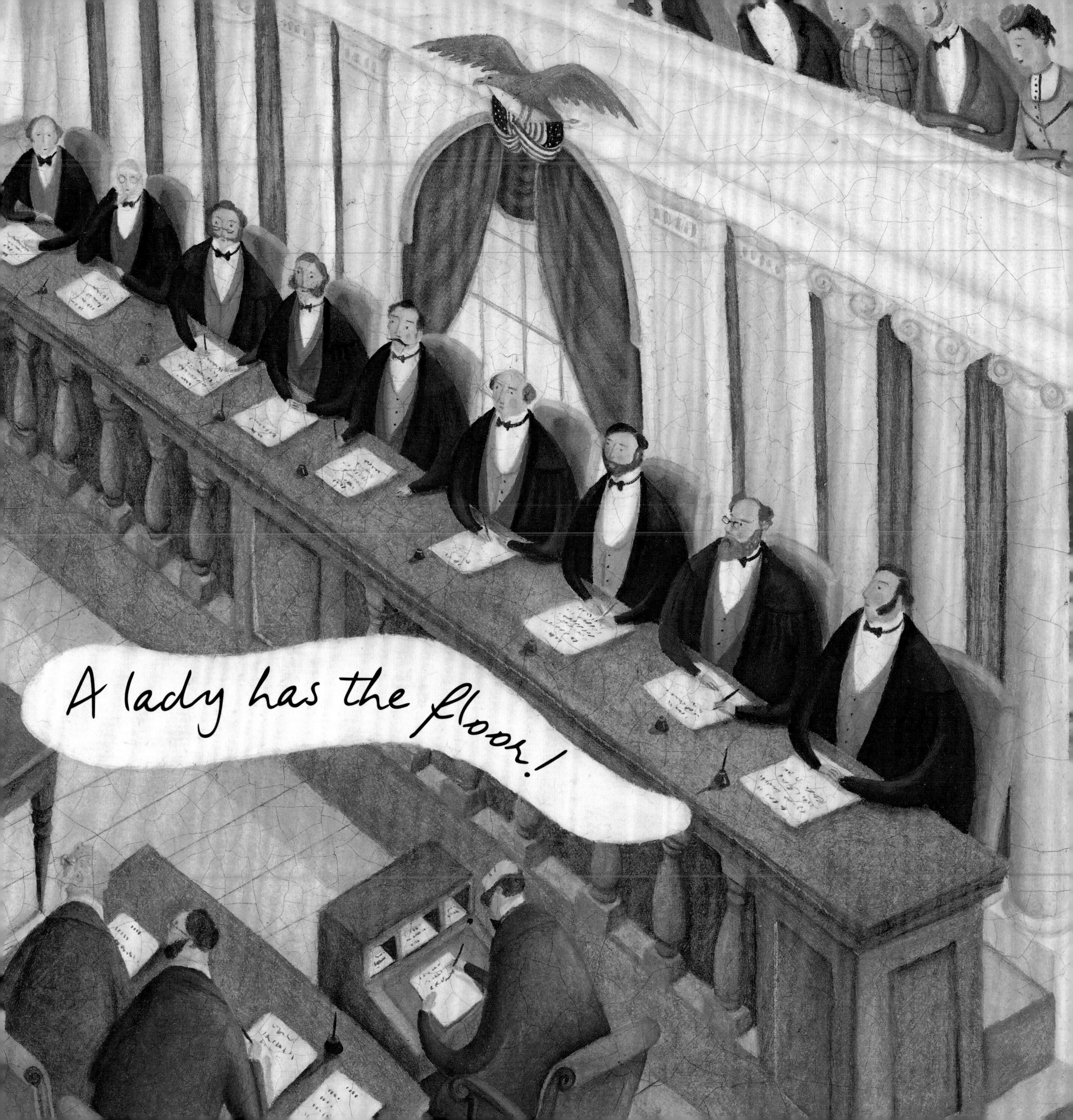
A lady has the floor!

Working in her office, Belva noticed men riding past on "horseless vehicles." They were getting to courtrooms faster than Belva, who walked or rode in her carriage. Never wanting to be left behind, Belva bought one of these contraptions for herself—and became the first woman to pedal around the nation's capital on a bicycle!

Mayors! Governors! Senators!

Belva spent every day fighting for equality, and she was determined to conquer another realm: the ballot box. She called for "women's suffrage"—the right to vote—and clamored for women's voices in laws and governing.

"Why not nominate women for important places? Is not Victoria Empress of India? Have we not among our country-women persons of as much talent and ability? Is not history full of precedents of women rulers?"

"It is quite time that we had our own party; our own platform, and our own nominees. We shall never have equal rights until we take them, nor respect until we command it."

As the 1884 presidential election grew closer, Belva lost patience with her old friends Susan B. Anthony and Elizabeth Cady Stanton. If women wanted to vote, they should seize the moment!

She mailed a letter to a women's newspaper, urging women to act. Editor Marietta Stow shared Belva's ideals. Having run for governor of California in 1882, Marietta was ready to see women enter political contests.

Marietta fired a letter right back! It said the National Equal Rights Party was nominating Belva for president and Marietta as her running mate. It was September, only two months until the election.

Belva got busy! She jumped onto trains and campaigned from town to town. "I cannot vote, but I can be voted for."

Her opponents got busy, too. Men paraded through the streets in bonnets and gowns, making fun of Belva. Newspapers said she dyed her hair, wore scarlet underwear while riding her bicycle—anything to embarrass her!

Belva ignored them and kept right on campaigning.

Bold!
Determined!
Strong!

"I never stopped fighting.
My cause was the cause of thousands of women."

BAKER

"I was ready to stand. It was not for the number of votes I should get. But for the chance to prove that a lady can be a candidate."

Equal Rights Ticket.

FOR PRESIDENT
BELVA A. LOCKWOOD.
FOR VICE-PRESIDENT
MARIETTA L. STOW.
1884

When Election Day arrived in November 1884, Belva's name was printed in clear letters—as strong a statement as any she'd made in classrooms and courtrooms. The first woman to appear on ballots for president, she received more than four thousand votes. It wasn't enough to beat Grover Cleveland for the White House, but it was enough to start people thinking.

Bold, determined, and strong,
Belva Bennett Lockwood was not afraid
to raise her own voice so that everyone—girls and boys, women and men,
African Americans and Native Americans, widows and veterans—
could be heard.

In the classroom! In the courtroom! In the White House!

This photograph of Belva Lockwood was taken between 1880 and 1890.

"I have not raised the dead, but I have awakened the living."

AUTHOR'S NOTE

Belva Lockwood spent her life fighting for equality, not just for women but for all people. Her clients often were outsiders—widows, veterans, Native Americans, former slaves—who, like Belva, had been denied their rights. One of her first acts before the U.S. Supreme Court in 1880 was to ask the court to admit Samuel R. Lowery, making him the first Southern African American lawyer to practice there.

In 1906, Belva argued on behalf of Native Americans in *Cherokee Nation v. United States.* The case involved members of the Eastern Cherokee Nation who were forced off their lands in North Carolina, Georgia, and Tennessee by the U.S. government in the 1830s. Thousands of Cherokees died along the grueling march west, known as "The Trail of Tears." Cherokee survivors wanted to recover the money owed for the sale of their lands. Belva argued that they deserved the full amount from the original sale, plus interest accrued over the following decades. She argued her case before the Supreme Court and won. The settlement was a staggering $5 million. Though Belva was more than seventy-five years old, she made trips to Oklahoma to ensure that every eligible Cherokee received a payment.

After running for president in 1884 and 1888, Belva turned her attention toward peace. She attended international peace conferences and was a nominating member of the Nobel Peace Prize committee. Even as a grandmother in her eighties, she traveled the world promoting a message of nonviolence.

When Belva Lockwood died on May 19, 1917, she had not yet seen her dream of women's suffrage come true. Within three years of her death, thirty-six states—a two-thirds majority—ratified the Nineteenth Amendment to the Constitution, granting all women in the United States the right to vote.

Now, every Election Day serves as a reminder that the freedoms we enjoy today are built upon the courage, determination, and hard work of remarkable women and men who came before us. Pioneers and reformers like Belva Lockwood, who dared to dream big and speak up for what they believed in, opened the door for women across the country to demand an education, an opportunity to lead, and the right for their voices to be heard.

TIMELINE

1830 October 24—Belva Ann Bennett born in Royalton, New York.

1848 Marries farmer Uriah McNall.

1849 Gives birth to daughter Lura.

1853 Uriah dies, leaving Belva a widow with a toddler to raise.

1854-57 Attends Genesee Wesleyan Seminary, then Genesee College, which later becomes Syracuse University; earns bachelor of science degree, graduating with honors; Lura lives with Belva's parents.

1857-66 Teaches at a variety of New York schools; introduces public speaking and physical exercise to girls.

1861-65 Civil War tears United States in two.

1866 Moves with Lura to Washington, D.C.; opens a private school for girls and boys.

1867 Founds Universal Franchise Association, which fights for women's right to vote.

1868 Marries Ezekiel Lockwood; gives birth to a second daughter, Jessie, the following year, who dies in infancy.

1869 Applies to law school but is told her presence is likely to distract the young men. National Woman Suffrage Association (NWSA) is founded, led by Susan B. Anthony and Elizabeth Cady Stanton; soon after, the American Woman Suffrage Association (AWSA) is formed by Lucy Stone, Henry Blackwell, and Julia Ward Howe. The two groups merge in 1890.

1870 The Fifteenth Amendment of the U.S. Constitution is ratified, granting African American men the right to vote.

1871 Attends National University Law School (which later becomes George Washington University Law School).

1872 Victoria Woodhull runs for president as Equal Rights Party candidate, though she faces steep challenges. She does not meet constitutionally mandated age requirement, does not appear on ballots, lacks funds to campaign, and spends Election Day in jail.

Susan B. Anthony and a dozen other women are arrested for voting in the presidential election.

1873 Belva completes law school coursework but is denied diploma; demands and later receives diploma from President Ulysses S. Grant.

1879 March 3—Sworn in as the first female member of the bar of the U.S. Supreme Court.

1880 February 2—Sponsors Samuel R. Lowery, African American attorney from the South, to practice before the U.S. Supreme Court.

November 30—Becomes the nation's first woman attorney to argue a case before the Supreme Court.

1884 June—Attends Republican National Convention; pushes for women's suffrage to be included in party's platform, but it is rejected.

September 3—Accepts nomination for president by National Equal Rights Party, with Marietta Stow, editor of the newspaper *Women's Herald of Industry*, as vice presidential candidate; party platform includes women's suffrage and equal rights for all. Belva becomes the first woman to launch a viable presidential campaign.

(cont'd)

(cont'd)

November 4—First woman to appear on ballots for president.

1885 Begins efforts for world peace.

1887 Susanna Salter of Argonia, Kansas, becomes the first woman in the United States elected mayor.

1888 Belva runs for president again as National Equal Rights Party candidate; Alfred Love is original running mate.

1890 Wyoming wins statehood, becoming the first state to allow its female citizens to vote.

1906 Belva goes before the U.S. Supreme Court to argue on behalf of the Eastern Cherokee Indians against the United States government; wins $5 million award for the tribe.

1916 Jeannette Rankin becomes the first woman elected to the U.S. Congress as a representative from Montana.

1917 May 19—Belva Lockwood dies in Washington, D.C., at age eighty-six.

1920 August 26—Eight days after ratification, the Nineteenth Amendment, granting all American women the right to vote, takes effect.

1924 Miriam "Ma" Ferguson of Texas and Nellie Tayloe Ross of Wyoming become the first women elected governors in the United States, in November. Nellie is first to be sworn into office, on January 5, 1925, about two weeks ahead of Miriam.

1932 Hattie Wyatt Caraway of Arkansas becomes the first woman elected to the U.S. Senate.

1933 Frances Perkins becomes the first woman appointed to a presidential cabinet post as secretary of labor under Franklin D. Roosevelt.

1972 Shirley Chisholm seeks Democratic nomination for president, becoming the first woman and first African American to run for the nomination of a major party.

1981 Sandra Day O'Connor becomes the first female justice of the U.S. Supreme Court, appointed by President Ronald Reagan.

1984 Geraldine Ferraro joins Democratic ticket with Walter Mondale, becoming the first female vice presidential candidate for a major American political party.

2016 Hillary Rodham Clinton becomes the first female presidential nominee of any major party. She wins the popular vote but loses the Electoral College.

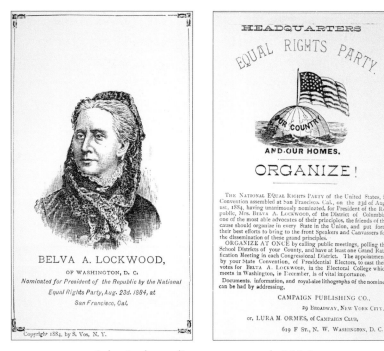

Belva Lockwood's campaign card, 1884

BIBLIOGRAPHY*

BOOKS AND PAPERS

Bly, Nellie. *Around the World in Seventy-Two Days and Other Writings*. Edited by Jean Marie Lutes. New York: Penguin Books, 2014.

Bozeman, Anne. "The Presidential Campaigns of Belva Lockwood." Undergraduate Research Awards, ScholarWorks@Georgia State University, Georgia State University Library, 2009. scholarworks.gsu.edu/univ_lib_ura/4.

Brown, Drollene P. *Belva Lockwood Wins Her Case*. Niles, IL: Albert Whitman, 1987.

Campbell, Karlyn Kohrs, ed. *Women Public Speakers in the United States, 1800–1925: A Bio-Critical Sourcebook*. Westport, CT: Greenwood, Press, 1993.

Cook, Frances A. "Belva Ann Lockwood: For Peace, Justice, and President." Stanford University Law School, Women's Legal History Biography Project, 1997. wlh-static.law.stanford.edu/papers/LockwoodB-Cook97.pdf.

Klebanow, Diana, and Franklin L. Jonas. *People's Lawyers: Crusaders for Justice in American History*. Armonk, NY: M. E. Sharpe, 2003.

Norgren, Jill. *Belva Lockwood: Equal Rights Pioneer*. Minneapolis: Twenty-First Century Books, 2009.

———. *Belva Lockwood: The Woman Who Would Be President*. New York: New York University Press, 2007.

Stern, Madeleine B. *We the Women: Career Firsts of Nineteenth-Century America*. New York: B. Franklin, 1974.

Whitman, Alden, ed. *American Reformers: An H. W. Wilson Biographical Dictionary*. New York: H. W. Wilson, 1985.

Winner, Julia Hull. *Belva A. Lockwood*. Lockport, NY: Niagara County Historical Society, 1969.

NEWSPAPERS AND MAGAZINES

Boston Daily Globe, December 22, 1884.
Chicago Daily Tribune, September 6, 1884.
Chicago Daily Tribune, November 10, 1884.
Chicago Daily Tribune, September 2, 1888.
Courier-Journal, September 18, 1884.
Life magazine, November 6, 1884.
Lippincott's Monthly Magazine, February 1888.
Los Angeles Times, September 3, 1893.
San Francisco Chronicle, May 20, 1917.
Washington Post, July 30, 1905.

SOURCE NOTES

The source of each quotation in this book is found below. The citation indicates the first words of the quotation and its document source. The document sources are listed in the bibliography.

"not afraid of snakes . . .": Lockwood, quoted in "Belva Lockwood: As a Little Girl She Could Walk a Rail Fence and Have a Dirty Face," *Los Angeles Times*, September 3, 1893.

"Has God given to one half . . .": Lockwood, quoted in Campbell, p. 45.

---

* Websites active at time of publication

"I believe that a woman . . .": Lockwood, quoted in "Cold Water and Politics," *Boston Daily Globe*, December 22, 1884.

"I always wanted an education . . .": Lockwood, quoted in "Belva A. Lockwood, Pioneer Woman Lawyer," *Washington Post*, July 30, 1905, p. A10.

"I was not to be squelched . . .": "My Efforts to Become a Lawyer" by Belva A. Lockwood, *Lippincott's Monthly Magazine*, February 1888.

"I have passed through . . .": same as above.

"Fight, fight, fight everlastingly . . .": Lockwood, quoted in Whitman, p. 529.

"Nothing was too daring . . .": "My Efforts to Become a Lawyer" by Belva A. Lockwood, *Lippincott's Monthly Magazine*, February 1888.

"Why not nominate . . .": letter from Lockwood to Marietta L. Stow, August 10, 1884, quoted in Winner, p. 129.

"It is quite time that we had . . .": same as above, p. 130.

"I cannot vote, but . . .": Lockwood, quoted in *Courier-Journal*, September 18, 1884.

"I never stopped fighting . . .": Lockwood, quoted in Campbell, p. 47.

"I was ready . . .": Lockwood, quoted in "Cold Water and Politics," *Boston Daily Globe*, December 22, 1884.

"I have not . . .": "My Efforts to Become a Lawyer" by Belva A. Lockwood, *Lippincott's Monthly Magazine*, February 1888.

ACKNOWLEDGMENTS

Special thanks to historian Rachel Walman of the New-York Historical Society for her keen insights.

For my mother and father, who taught me to read and to dream
—KH

For Biddy Macfarlane, who rose through the judicial system to become one of Great Britain's first female judges. Thank you, Biddy, for being such a wonderful neighbor, friend, and inspiration.
—AJ

Text copyright © 2018 by Kate Hannigan
Illustrations copyright © 2018 by Alison Jay
All rights reserved.

For information about permission to reproduce selections from this book, please contact permissions@highlights.com.

Calkins Creek
An Imprint of Highlights
815 Church Street
Honesdale, Pennsylvania 18431
Printed in China

ISBN: 978-1-62979-453-2

Library of Congress Control Number: 2017942219

First edition

10 9 8 7 6 5 4 3 2 1

Designed by Barbara Grzeslo
Production by Sue Cole
Text set in Bulmer
The illustrations are done with Alkyd paint (a quick drying oil paint) with crackle varnish.

Picture Credits: Library of Congress Prints and Photographs Division: LC-BH834-55: p. 28; Granger, NYC: p. 30.